BREEDERS' BEST
A KENNEL CLUB BOOK

Dalmatian

By Susan Brooksbank

Emily Hoffman

BREEDERS' BEST

A KENNEL CLUB BOOK®

DALMATIAN

ISBN: 1-59378-925-4

Copyright © 2004

Kennel Club Books, Inc.
308 Main Street, Allenhurst, NJ 07711 USA
Printed in South Korea

PHOTOS BY:
Paulette Braun, Isabelle Français,
Carol Ann Johnson,
and Bernd Brinkmann.

DRAWINGS BY:
Yolyanko el Habanero

Contents

Meet the Dalmatian

T he history of the "Firehouse Dog," the stylish Dalmatian, is as varied and interesting as his spotted coat. This aristocratic dog's ancestry spans several centuries and includes many different roles. While he is best known in the modern world as the official mascot of the firefighter, the breed's heritage includes many diverse occupations and crosses the continents of Europe, Asia and Africa.

The Dalmatian, or "Dal," as we call him affectionately, has served humanity for hundreds of years in many ways. Today his talents prove useful for assistance work with the handicapped, along with other roles.

Although his official beginnings remain the subject of much dispute, centuries-old paintings, writings and engravings depict Dalmatian-type dogs in various scenarios, confirming his use as a multi-purpose canine. The spotted dog that worked with horses dates as far back as the Middle Ages. Tracing further back, Dalmatian look-alikes are depicted running beside the chariots of ancient Egypt.

The Dal has performed in circuses, on TV and on the big screen. The *101 Dalmatians* book and subsequent films brought the Dal into the limelight and created a huge demand for the breed.

Historians have placed the Dalmatian in a variety of other roles throughout past centuries: shepherd, ratter and vermin dog, trail hound, stag and boar hunter and the more familiar circus dog that performed tricks and enter-tained audiences under the big top. Some authorities wrote of spotted dogs who were employed as sentinels on the borders of

The Dal is most famous as a firehouse dog. Before motorized engines, the Dal would run with the horse-drawn fire wagons, barking along the way to clear the road.

Dalmatia, once a province of Austria on the eastern shore off the coast of Venice, hence the breed's name. (If you remember that the "Dalmatian" comes from "Dalmatia," you'll never misspell the breed name again!) Several colorful legends tell of Dalmatian-type dogs traveling with bands of gypsies across Eastern Europe. Whatever the role, one fact remains. In every task assigned to him, the Dalmatian was a tireless worker whose intelligence and willingness to please served his master well.

After his introduction to 17th-century Great Britain, the Dalmatian continued to ply his ancient carriage trade. A stout guardian to travelers, he trotted beside the horse-drawn carriages on long journeys to protect the passengers from dangerous highwaymen. Later the Dal was adopted by the British aristocracy who utilized the dog as an ornament for their fancy carriages, with the Dal running beside the horses and uniformed drivers. Sometimes sent ahead of the coaches to clear the way, the Dal "coached" under the rear or front axle of the carriage, his spotted coat adding distinction to the ornate trappings and the liverymen.

The Dalmatian was popular also with the British commoner, and soon became a trademark of the fire station, galloping ahead of the horse-drawn water wagons. The athletic Dal was swift enough to keep up with the wagons, and the contrast of his spotted coat made him easier to see in twilight hours.

After his migration to the United States, the Dalmatian continued in the role of "Firehouse Dog," working alongside the horses and standing guard over fire stations. The Dalmatian's regal bearing has changed little over the centuries. He is, above all, a gentleman, a quiet fellow with a discerning eye. He is reserved and courteous with strangers, but his guardian instincts remain strong and he is always ready to defend his family if necessary. The modern Dal also has retained his penchant for performing, which is reflected in his need to work and exceeded only by his love of whatever task he may be doing. Love, in fact, may be his most distin-

The Dalmatian has long been associated with accompanying and guarding horse-drawn carriages or individual horseback riders.

guishing characteristic, as his work ethic is surpassed only by his great capacity for friendship.

MEET THE DALMATIAN

Overview

- The exact origins of the Dalmatian are a mystery, although evidence of similar dogs date back to ancient Egypt.
- The Dalmatian's many talents and trainability have enabled him to assist man in various capacities, including as a guard dog, a protector of horse-drawn carriages, a hunter and an entertainer.
- The Dalmatian is very athletic and possesses great endurance, able to trot for long distances.
- The Dalmatian is still known in many countries as the "Firehouse Dog."

Description of the Dalmatian

A breed standard is a breeder's testimony of love and dedication to his chosen breed of dog. Indeed, standards are contemplated, written and revised by knowledgeable breed people through the national breed club, the Dalmatian Club of America (DCA), in order to preserve the pure ancestral qualities of each breed. The current Dalmatian breed standard, approved by the American Kennel Club (AKC) in 1989, bears witness to the spotted coaching dog of the Middle Ages and beyond.

The spirit and substance of the Dalmatian is captured best in the first

The "snowflake" of the dog world, the Dalmatian is never spotted exactly like another.

paragraph of the standard: "The Dalmatian is a distinctively spotted dog; poised and alert; strong and muscular; free of shyness; intelligent in expression; symmetrical in outline; and without exaggeration or coarseness. The Dalmatian is capable of great endurance, combined with a fair amount of speed."

The Dal's muscular, compact body should not be exaggerated in any way. He should look like a lean athlete in top condition.

The Dal's spots are, of course, his most distinguishing feature and are critical points in the breed's evaluation. The ground color is pure white, and spots may be black or liver-colored, with any other color a disqualification. The size and shape of the spots are most important. They should be round and well-defined, vary in size from the size of a dime to a half dollar and be evenly distributed, including on the head, legs, tail and ears. Patches of color are disqualifications. The coat is short, dense, fine and close-fitting, never woolly or silky, yet sleek and glossy in appearance.

"Poised and alert"—this photo says it all!

Dalmatian

Height for both sexes ranges from 19 to 23 inches at the withers, with size deviation faulted. Oversize is a disqualification, and any dog or bitch over 24 inches is disqualified.

The Dalmatian's body is sleek and muscular, having good substance and sturdy bone. The Dal's overall conformation bears witness to his coaching heritage, reflecting his great endurance and

The height range for the Dalmatian is between 19 and 23 inches, allowing for noticeable size differences among members of the breed.

ability to travel long distances by foot. The body's outline is fairly square, with forequarters smoothly muscled and hindquarters powerful with

front and rear feet are round and compact, with thick elastic pads and well-arched toes.

In keeping with the Dalmatian's historical use as a

Most Dalmatians today do not have regular opportunities to work or run long distances, so owners must find ways to keep their Dals active. Agility training and competition are terrific outlets for Dalmatians' energy, and they certainly are a sight to see in action.

well-defined muscles, reflecting the breed's affinity for lengthy runs.

The standard states that a Dal's feet are very important, as well they would be for any long-distance runner. Both

coaching dog, the breed's gait and endurance are of great importance. Movement is steady and effortless, with the Dal's powerful muscle and good condition producing smooth, effortless action.

Dalmatian

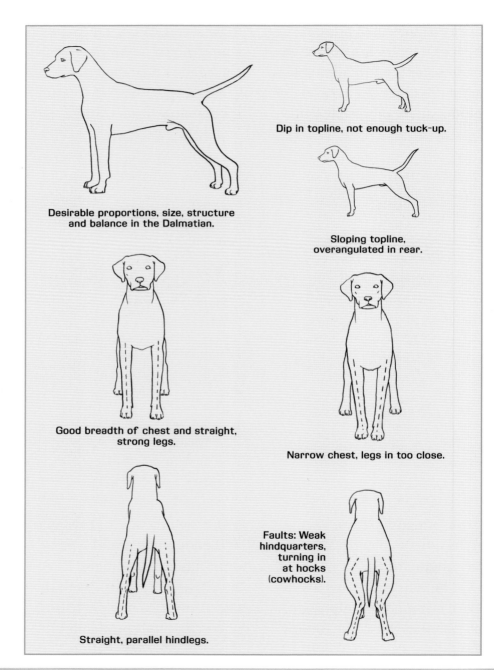

Desirable proportions, size, structure and balance in the Dalmatian.

Dip in topline, not enough tuck-up.

Sloping topline, overangulated in rear.

Good breadth of chest and straight, strong legs.

Narrow chest, legs in too close.

Straight, parallel hindlegs.

Faults: Weak hindquarters, turning in at hocks (cowhocks).

The Dal's head is of fair length, the skin taut, and his expression is alert and intelligent, indicating a stable and outgoing temperament. The eyes are round and moderate in size. Brown eyes are desirable, darker preferred. Blue eyes are acceptable in the US but not in the United Kingdom.

Temperament is described twice in the standard, thus emphasizing stable and outgoing, yet dignified, personality, and indicating the importance of those qualities in the breed. Shyness is noted as a major fault.

In some cases, temperament has been sadly compromised since the mid-1990s, thanks to the "live action" *101 Dalmatians* movie and sequels, and the breed's subsequent rise in popularity and overbreeding. Poorly bred Dals are often hyper and aggressive and suffer a multitude of health problems. Prospective buyers should seek out *only* reputable breeders for properly bred Dalmatian pups.

DESCRIPTION OF THE DALMATIAN

Overview

- The breed standard, devised by the parent club, describes the ideal Dalmatian, detailing physical conformation as well as character and movement.
- The Dalmatian's body should by sleek and muscular. The feet should be compact, befitting a long-distance runner.
- The Dal's most recognizable feature is his spotted coat. The standard specifies size and distribution of the trademark spots.
- Temperament is mentioned twice in the standard, stressing its importance. Knowledgeable, reputable breeders place sound temperament and good health as top priorities in their breeding programs.

Are You a Dalmatian Person?

First and foremost, a prospective owner must be sure he can provide the Dal with plenty of time and space for exercise to keep the dog physically and mentally fit.

Endurance could well be the Dalmatian's middle name. This dog is a true road warrior, having for centuries run alongside horses, carriages and fire wagons. The breed's history as a performance animal, working at myriad difficult tasks, has etched stamina deep into his character and he is programmed for action. The Dal is a dog that can travel many, many miles without tiring; thus, his need for exercise is huge. After centuries of employment, this dog will not be satisfied with a life of inactivity.

Throughout his history, the Dalmatian also has demonstrated remarkable intelligence tempered with a willingness to do his master's bidding. These combined qualities create training challenges for anyone who adds this spotted athlete to his family. Bluntly put, living with a Dalmatian is a lot of work.

Despite these challenges, a well-bred Dalmatian is indeed an excellent family dog. He is highly affectionate and needs to be with his human family. He is loving and patient with children if he is properly socialized with them at an early age, and is sturdy enough to tolerate child's play, although all play should be supervised by an adult. That said, children also must be taught how to properly behave around their dogs, whether puppy or adult.

The Dal is an excellent watchdog

The best time for Dals is time spent with their owners, and the feeling is mutual!

As active as he is, the Dalmatian still appreciates the comforts of home and enjoys curling up for some quiet time.

and views strangers with a most discerning eye. He prefers to maintain a mannerly distance as he watches protectively over his master and human family. He is never threatening or aggressive unless his instincts warn him of some danger, and he will bark when he senses something is awry.

The Dal gets along well with other animals, and his affinity for horses has continued into the 21st-century. For years the St. Louis-based Anheuser Busch brewing company used Dalmatians to protect their horses and guard their delivery wagons. Today their dogs ride atop the wagons, entertaining the crowds at parades, festivals and major sporting events.

Young Dals can become difficult when they enter the "terrible twos" of adolescence. Training and socialization are essential to teach manners and acceptable behavior. Puppy classes, basic obedience and daily training sessions are excellent outlets for the breed's tremendous energy. Mental stimulation is equally important or the Dal will become bored and creatively destructive. Dals live best with people who are physically active and who maintain a lifestyle in which a dog is included and always welcome. A securely fenced yard is necessary, given the Dal's proclivity to run. The breed's average lifespan is 11 to 13 years.

The short Dalmatian coat requires minimal care but shedding is a year-round problem, and the short hair sticks to everything, making the term "easykeeper" an oxymoron. Fussy housekeepers, beware.

Today the "Firehouse Dog" distinction may be eclipsed only by the image of Disney's *101 Dalmatians* running down the street. The re-release of the original 1961 animated film caused the breed's popularity to skyrocket in 1991, creating a huge demand for Dal puppies. Unfortunately, irresponsible breeders responded to this demand. The DCA was better-prepared for the 1996 release of the live-animal release of the movie, which thus did not have much effect on the breed.

This created a corresponding problem for humane societies and Dalmatian rescue groups when those cute pups grew into highly energetic adolescents who were as wild and disobedient as the movie pups, and unprepared owners abandoned their Dals to shelters and breed rescues.

If you fancy living with a Dalmatian, patronize only a knowledgeable, ethical breeder who will educate you about the ups and downs of this intriguing breed and who can counsel you during all stages of the dog's life.

Road-trial competitions develop your Dal's natural instincts and endurance, allowing him to put his innate skills to the test.

ARE YOU A DALMATIAN PERSON?

Overview

- The Dalmatian person is ready and able to provide proper training and lots of activity for this intelligent, energetic dog, who can bore easily without sufficient mental stimulation.
- The Dalmatian person has time to care for his dog and can provide ample accommodations.
- The Dalmatian person is responsible and available, for this dog wants to spend as much time doing things with his owner as possible.
- The Dalmatian person actively pursues his dog's education.

Selecting a Dalmatian Breeder

You must find a breeder who truly loves the Dalmatian and who puts the welfare of the breed first.

A s with any major purchase, *where* you buy is as important as *what* you buy. The *101 Dalmatians* movies created a huge demand for adorable spotted Dalmatian puppies and spawned a corresponding increase in poor-quality Dalmatians bred to capitalize on the breed's sudden explosion in popularity. As a result, Dal health and temperament suffered accordingly.

Only a responsible breeder can provide a healthy, stable pup that is well suited to your family and lifestyle. Puppy mills, brokers and uninformed breeders are for-profit operations that care only about the bottom-line dollar and not about the quality of the dogs they mass-produce. Whatever your reason for wanting a Dal pup…companionship, dog shows, agility trials or obedience competition… you want a healthy dog with an excellent temperament, and a reputable breeder is the only logical place to "shop."

Locating a good breeder can be an emotionally trying experience, taxing your patience and your willpower. All puppies are adorable and it's easy to fall in love with the first cute pup you see, but a poorly bred Dalmatian may have health and temperament problems that can break your heart and empty your wallet. (Avoid temptation…do not visit that "doggie in the window.") Research the breed and breeders before you visit litters.

Take a look around the breeder's premises and meet all of his dogs. Outdoor kennel runs should be spacious and clean, just like any area in which dogs or pups are kept.

The litter's first interaction with humans is with the breeder. By handling the pups and spending time with them, the breeder provides essential early socialization, so important in the pups' future relationships with their owners and other people.

Arm yourself with a list of questions for the breeder (a good one will expect that). Then leave your checkbook and your kids at home so you aren't tempted to buy the first puppy you see, no matter how irresistible.

For starters, ask to see the pedigree and registration papers. The pedigree should include three to five generations of ancestry. Inquire about any titles in the pedigree. Titles indicate a dog's accomplishments in some area of conformation or performance competition, which proves the merits of the ancestors and adds to the breeder's credibility. While it is true that a pedigree is no guarantee of health or breed quality, it is still a good insurance policy.

Ask the breeder why he planned this litter. A good breeder should explain the genetics behind this particular breeding and what he expects the breeding to produce. He never breeds because "his

Dalmatian is sweet and/or beautiful, his neighbor's dog is handsome, they will have lovely puppies," and so on. Just loving his dog like crazy does not qualify an individual to breed dogs intelligently or to raise a litter of Dalmatian pups properly.

Ask about health clearances. Dalmatians are prone to deafness, with a small percentage of Dals born deaf in both ears. Responsible breeders breed only hearing dogs and test all pups for deafness. Using the breed-approved Brainstem Auditory Evoked Response (BAER) testing system, they test the litter's hearing status after four weeks of age and euthanize any pups that are totally deaf. Dals who are deaf in only one ear make fine pets but probably should not be bred.

Dalmatians are also prone to urinary-tract problems due to the high levels of uric acid excreted in their urine, which can cause the formation of kidney and bladder stones. Dal owners can avoid these problems by feeding a diet low in protein and purines, restricting red meat and other high-protein table food, and providing a plentiful water supply. Some Dal owners offer only distilled water to their dogs. Your Dalmatian breeder should address this issue and recommend an appropriate diet.

While not proven to be a genetic disorder, Dalmatians also tend to have allergies, with some affected by a skin disorder that Dal fanciers sometimes call "Dal crud." To date, the best known method of producing unaffected dogs is to remove visibly affected dogs from a breeding program. Certainly not a cure by any means, but most conscientious breeders do not include chronically allergic dogs in their breeding stock.

Ask the breeder if the sire and dam have hip clearances from the OFA (Orthopedic Foundation for Animals) or PennHIP® (the University of Pennsylvania's Hip

Improvement Program), proving them free of hip dysplasia. Has the breeder done thyroid testing and eye testing (the latter registration by CERF, the Canine Eye Registration Foundation) on the

Dalmatians can have large litters, and caring for this many pups certainly requires dedication to the breed, careful attention to each pup and a good sense of humor!

sire and dam? Good breeders will gladly, in fact, proudly, provide these documents. For more information on genetic disorders in Dalmatians, you can check with the Dalmatian Club of America's website at www.thedca.org.

Experienced breeders are frequently involved in some aspect of the dog fancy with their dog(s), perhaps showing or training them for some type of performance event or other dog-related activity. Their Dalmatian(s) may have earned titles in various areas of canine competition, which is added proof of their experience and commitment to the breed.

Dedicated breeders should belong to the Dalmatian Club of America (DCA) and perhaps an area breed or kennel club. Such affiliation with other experienced breeders and sportsmen

Pet dog, show dog, coaching dog...herding dog? Not one of the breed's traditional roles, but this Dal seems right at home with his color-coordinated bovine friends.

expands their knowledge of the breed and breed characteristics, which further enhances a breeder's credibility. Responsible breeders, by the way, do not raise several different breeds of dog or produce multiple litters of pups throughout the year; one or two litters a year is typical. Some

major kennels may offer several litters annually, but they are wealthy operations that are well equipped to properly raise and socialize their pups.

The breeder will ask you questions, too… about your dog history, previous dogs you have owned, what breeds and what became of them. He will want to know the specifics of your living arrangements, e.g., house, yard, kids, other pets, etc., your goals for this pup (showing, pet, performance events) and how you plan to raise him. The breeder's primary concern is the future of his puppies and whether you and your family are suitable owners who will provide a proper and loving home for his precious little one. Avoid any breeder who agrees to sell you a Dalmatian puppy without any type of interrogation process. Such indifference indicates a lack of concern about the pups and casts doubt on the breeder's ethics and breeding program.

A good breeder should also warn you about the downside of the Dalmatian. No breed of dog is perfect, nor is every breed suitable for every person's temperament and lifestyle. Dals are high-energy dogs who crave lots of action. Simply put, they are a lot of work, and the breeder should be honest with you. Be prepared to weigh the good news against the bad about the Dalmatian.

Most Dalmatian breeders have puppy sales contracts that include specific health guarantees and reasonable return policies. Your breeder should agree to accept a puppy back if things do not work out. The breeder also should be willing, indeed anxious, to check up on the puppy's progress after he leaves home. The breeder should be available if you have questions or if problems arise with the pup.

Breeders can place their pet-quality puppies on what is called the AKC Limited Regis-

tration. This registers the pup with the AKC and allows him to compete in AKC-licensed competitions, but does not allow the registration of any offspring from the mature dog. The purpose of Limited Registration is to prevent indiscrim-

Is the breeder active in showing her dogs? If your pup's pedigree shows many ancestors with conformation titles, your odds of his growing into a dog with real potential in the ring are greater.

inate breeding of "pet-quality" Dalmatians. The breeder, and only the breeder, can cancel the limited registration if the adult dog develops into breeding quality. For pups with no breeding potential, breeders will contractually require the owner to have the pup spayed or neutered at the appropriate age, ensuring that physical or health defects are not passed on.

Feel free to ask for references…and check them out. It's unlikely that a breeder will offer names of unhappy puppy clients, but calling other owners may make you more comfortable dealing with a particular breeder. Check with the AKC (www.akc.org) and DCA for breeder referrals in your area. Their websites offer links to clubs and breeders throughout the US. Any bit of information gleaned from owners and fanciers will make you a smarter shopper when

you visit a litter of pups.

The end result? You can expect to pay a dear price for all of these breeder qualities, whether you fancy a pet-quality Dalmatian for a companion dog or one with show or performance potential. The discount or bargain Dalmatian is not a bargain at all. Indeed, the discount pup is a potential disaster that has little chance of developing into a healthy, stable adult. Such bargains could ultimately cost you a fortune in vet expenses and heartache that can't be measured in dollars and cents.

So how do you find a reputable breeder you can trust? Do your puppy homework before you visit litters. Spend the day at a dog show or other dog event where you can meet breeders and exhibitors and get to know their dogs. Most Dalmatian fanciers are more than happy to show off their dogs and brag about their accomplishments. If you know a Dalmatian you are fond

Choose your pup wisely, and he will grow into a well-rounded, active, loyal canine companion beyond compare. A true man's— or woman's— best friend!

of, ask the owner where he got his dog. You also can ask a local vet for possible referrals.

Skip the puppy ads in your local newspaper. Reputable breeders rarely advertise in newspapers. They are very particular about prospective puppy owners and do not rely on mass advertising to attract the right people. Rather, they depend on referrals from other breeders and previous puppy clients. They are more than willing to keep any puppy past the usual eight-week placement age until the right person comes along.

Observe all dogs on the breeder's premises. The breeder will be happy to show you her beautiful champions!

Aside from careful research, perhaps the second most important ingredient in your breeder search is patience. You will not likely find the right breeder or litter on your first go-around. Breeders often have waiting lists, but a good Dalmatian pup is worth the wait.

SELECTING A DALMATIAN BREEDER

Overview

- To find a reputable breeder, write, phone or email the AKC or the Dalmatian Club of America for contacts.
- Visit a dog show to meet breeders and handlers of good dogs.
- Know what to expect from a quality breeder and be patient in your search.
- Ask about pedigrees, sales agreements, health clearances, registration papers and references.
- The breeder should inform you about the incidence of hip dysplasia, deafness, urinary-tract and skin problems and other hereditary conditions in his line.

Finding the Right Puppy

If you plan to live with an active, high-energy breed like the Dalmatian, finding the right pup is important to your long-term success and happiness together. A good breeder can help you select a pup that will best suit your goals and lifestyle.

You may have to travel to visit a good litter, but up-close and personal is the only way to choose your pup. That way, you can become better acquainted with the breeder and the mother of the pups, and the environment in which the pups are

On a very young litter, you can barely see the spots. The spots grow and develop along with the pup.

raised. If possible, visit more than one litter and keep notes on what you see and like…and don't like…about each one. Your research will pay off.

Where and how a litter of pups is raised is vitally important to the pups' early development into confident and social animals. The litter should be kept indoors, preferably in the house or in an adjoining sheltered area, not isolated in a basement or outdoor kennel. Puppies need to be socialized daily with people and people activities. The greater their exposure to household sights and sounds between three to four weeks and seven weeks of age, the easier their adjustment will be to their future human family.

During your visit, scrutinize the puppies as well as their living area for cleanliness and signs of sickness or poor health. The pups should be reasonably clean (allowing for normal non-stop "puppy-pies"). They should appear energetic, bright-eyed and

Follow the leader! The kids are all lined up and ready to explore with Mom.

Meeting the litter and spending time getting to know each puppy is an exciting and informative part of the selection process.

alert. Healthy pups have clean, shiny coats, are well proportioned and feel solid and muscular without being overly fat and pot-bellied. Watch for crusted eyes or nose and any watery discharge from the nose, eyes or ears. Check for evidence of watery or bloody stools.

Visit with the dam and the sire, if possible. In many cases, the sire is not on premises, but the breeder should have photos and a résumé of his character- istics and accomplishments. It is normal for some dams to be somewhat protective of their young, but overly aggressive behavior is unacceptable. Temperament is inherited, and if one or both parents are aggressive or very shy, it is likely that some of the pups will inherit those characteristics. The breeder should have a number of older dogs in the kennel, as this shows that

he has been in the breed for a while and has the experience of five or six generations of his line.

Dalmatian puppies are born pure white, with the spots beginning to fill in during the first few weeks. No two Dalmatians are spotted identically; thus, each Dalmatian is unique. For show purposes, the number of spots is not as important as their evenness of distribution. Spots may be black or liver-colored, but not both colors on the same dog.

Notice how the pups interact with their litter- mates and their surround- ings, especially their response to people. They should be active and outgoing. In many litters, some pups will be more outgoing than others, but even a quiet pup that is properly socialized should not be shy or spooky and should not shrink from a friendly voice or outstretched hand.

The breeder should be honest in discussing any differences in puppy personalities. Although most personality. The breeder's observations are valuable aids in selecting a puppy that will be compatible with you and your lifestyle.

Tell the breeder if you

These napping pups make quite a pile of snoozing spots!

breeders do some type of temperament testing, they also spend the pups' first eight weeks or so cuddling them and cleaning up after them. By the time the litter is ready for visitors, the breeder knows the subtle differences in each pup's wish to show your pup in conformation or compete in other events. Some pups will show more promise than others, and he can help you select one that will best suit your long-term goals.

Do you prefer a male or female? Which one is right

for you? Both sexes are loving and loyal, and the differences are due more to individual personalities rather than gender. Some people believe that the Dalmatian female is a gentler soul and easier to live with. Like many females, she also can be a bit more moody, depending on her whims and hormonal peaks. She may also be a bit shorter, standing between 19 and 21 inches at her withers and weighing between 40 to 50 pounds.

The male is often a couple of inches taller than the female and overall bigger and more powerful. Although males tend to be more even-tempered than

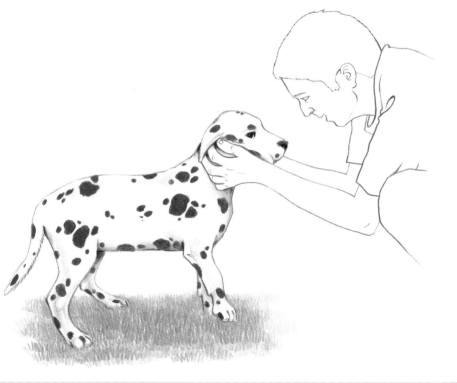

When visiting the litter, the pups should approach you and be eager to meet you, as well as be amenable to petting and handling.

Because of the genetic problems seen in the Dal, breeders must breed only healthy, sound dogs to produce healthy, sound puppies.

bitches, they are also more physical and exuberant during adolescence, which can be problematic in a high-energy, powerful dog. An untrained male can also become dominant with people and other dogs. A solid foundation in obedience is necessary if you want your Dal pup to respect you as his leader.

Intact males tend to be more territorial, especially with other male dogs. In males, both testicles should be descended into the scrotum. A dog with undescended testicles will make a fine pet, but will be ineligible to compete in the show ring.

Neutering or spaying your Dal will create a level

playing field and eliminate most of those gender differences.

By eight weeks of age, the pups should have had their hearing tested, have been wormed several times, have had the first puppy shot and have a vet's certificate verifying good health at the time of the exam. Front dewclaws may be removed, usually at three to five days old, but removal is not required by the standard.

The breeder should tell you what the pup has been eating, when and how much. Some send home a

Pups learn the ways of the canine world by playing and interacting with their littermates, posturing for position in the puppy pack.

Imagine the effort behind this photo: getting this many Dalmatian puppies to stay still!

small supply of puppy food to mix with your own during the first few days. Most breeders also give their clients a puppy "take-home" packet which includes a copy of the health certificate, the puppy's pedigree and registration papers, copies of the parents' health clearances, the breeder's sales contract and a diet sheet. Many supply literature on the breed and how to properly raise and train a Dalmatian. Dedicated breeders know that the more owners know, the better life will be for their precious pups.

FINDING THE RIGHT PUPPY

Overview

- Visit the litter to see the puppies up close and personal. You are seeking healthy, sound puppies with good hearing and sound temperaments.
- Trust the breeder whom you've selected to recommend a puppy that fits your lifestyle and personality.
- Decide upon a male or a female puppy based on gender-related personality and physical differences.
- Evaluate the kennel environment for overall cleanliness and signs of good health.
- Meet the dam and the sire, if possible, and evaluate their temperament and overall appearance.

Welcoming the Dalmatian

As with a new baby, there is much to do prior to bringing your Dalmatian puppy home. This is a major life event, and a thorough preparation beforehand will ease the pup's transition from his canine family to his new human world.

Stock up on puppy supplies from a pet-supply store or catalog and puppy-proof the house before your pup comes home. You won't have time after he arrives. A thorough puppy-proofing will prevent any accidents or surprises that could be

The pups start out with the best possible nutrition by nursing from their mother.

dangerous and even fatal for your pup. It will also preserve your property and your peace of mind.

Puppy shopping is the fun part, but hang on to your purse strings. Puppy stuff, especially the non-essentials, is often too cute to resist, so "stocking up" can easily decimate your budget. Start with basic essentials and save the puppy goodies until later.

We're ready! Dalmatian pups leave the breeder no earlier than eight weeks of age.

FEEDING VESSELS

You'll need two separate serving pieces, one for food and one for water. Stainless steel pans are your best choices as they are chew-proof and easy to clean. Dalmatians have powerful jaws and love to chew. Aluminum and many plastics are much too flimsy. Plastic dishes retain bacteria that can give the pup a rash around the mouth, and those cute ceramic bowls break easily. Tip-proof is

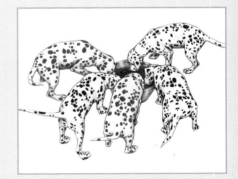

The pups are weaned and the breeder starts them on solid food. You should begin by feeding your pup the same diet he was getting from the breeder.

35

a good idea, since most puppies love to splash about in their water bowls, and the Dal pup is no exception. Ask your vet if you should elevate his food and water bowls. There is debate about this, but some believe that it helps to prevent a deadly condition known as bloat. Ask your vet about the condition and other simple daily preventatives.

Stainless steel bowls are preferable for the Dalmatian. Plastic bowls may retain bacteria and cause a rash on the puppy's mouth.

PUPPY FOOD

Your Dalmatian pup should be fed a quality food that is appropriate for his age and breed. Most quality dog foods now offer specific formulas that address the nutritional needs of small, medium (your Dalmatian) and large breeds of dog during the various stages of their lives. Dalmatians grow rapidly and need a well-balanced food to keep their joints healthy during that first year of rapid growth. Feed a good-quality medium-breed growth food, which should be his diet for his first year. After that, you can switch to a medium-breed adult-maintenance dog food.

Your Dalmatian's early growth period as well as his long-term health will benefit from a diet of high-quality puppy and dog food. The Dalmatian breed has a unique uric acid metabolism, with high levels of uric acid excreted in the urine, making kidney and bladder stone formation a possibility. A low-protein, low-purine diet with no red meat is strongly advised to help prevent that problem. For experienced recommendations, check with your breeder and your vet before you buy your puppy's food.

Many breed fanciers indulge their passion for spots with Dal-inspired accessories for their dogs...and even sometimes for themselves!

COLLARS AND ID TAGS

Your Dalmatian pup should have an adjustable collar that will expand to fit him as he grows. Lightweight nylon adjustable collars work best for both pups and adult dogs. To fit properly, you should be able to slip two fingers between the collar and your puppy's neck. The ID tag should have your phone number, name and address, but *not* the puppy's name, as that would enable a stranger to identify and call your dog. Some owners include a line that says "Dog needs medication," to hopefully speed the dog's return if he is lost or stolen. Put the collar on as soon as the pup comes home so he can get used to wearing it. It's best to use an "O" ring for the tag, as the "S" ring snags on carpets and comes off easily.

Also ask your vet about microchipping, a painless procedure that inserts a tiny chip under the dog's skin between the shoulder blades. The chip contains an ID number and your contact information, and can be scanned if the dog is found.

Today, even dog collars have gone high-tech. Some come equipped with beepers and tracking devices. The most advanced pet identification tool uses a Global Positioning System and fits inside a collar or tag. When your dog leaves his programmed home perimeter, the device sends a message directly to your phone or email address.

Choke collars and pinch collars are for training purposes and should be worn only during training sessions, used only by those who know how to use them properly. Training collars should never be used on Dalmatian puppies under 16 weeks of age.

LEASHES

For your own convenience and for puppy's safety, his leash wardrobe should

Start your Dal puppy off with a lightweight buckle collar and nylon lead. You will need a larger collar and stronger lead as the dog grows.

include at least two kinds of leads. A narrow 6-foot flat nylon or leather leash is best for walks, puppy kindergarten and other obedience classes. The other lead is called a "flexi" lead. The "flexi" is an extendable lead housed in a large handle. It extends and retracts with the push of a button. This is the ideal tool for exercising and should be a staple in every puppy's wardrobe. Flexis are available in several lengths (8 feet to 26 feet) and strengths, depending on breed size. Longer is better, as it allows your dog to run safely about and check out the good sniffing areas farther away from you. They are especially handy for exercising your puppy in unfenced areas or when traveling with your dog.

BEDDING
Dog beds are just plain fun. Beds run the gamut from small and inexpensive to elegant, high-end beds

suitable for the most royal of dog breeds. However, don't go overboard just yet. Better to save that fancy bed for when your Dalmatian is older and less apt to shred it up or make a puddle on it. For puppy bedding, it's best to use a large towel, mat or blanket that can be easily laundered (which will probably be often).

The crate you purchase for the pup should be large enough for the adult. A wire crate allows the dog to see what's going on around him, perfect for the Dal!

CRATES AND GATES

These will be your most important puppy purchases. A crate is your most valuable tool for house-breaking your pup, and his favorite place to feel secure. Crates come in three varieties: wire, fabric mesh and the more familiar plastic, airline-type crate. Wire or fabric crates offer the best ventilation and some conveniently fold up suitcase-style. A fabric-mesh crate might be a little risky for the Dalmatian youngster who likes to dig and chew. Whatever your choice, purchase an adult-sized crate, about 26-27 inches high, 24 inches wide and 36 inches long. Your Dalmatian pup will soon grow into it. Crates are available at most pet stores and through pet-supply catalogs.

A well-placed baby gate will protect your house from the inevitable puppy mischief, and thus save your sanity as well. It's wise to confine your puppy to a tiled or uncarpeted room or space, one that is accessible to the outside door he will use for potty trips. Gated to a safe area where he cannot wreak havoc or destruction, your puppy will soon master Housebreaking 101, learn to chew only appropriate chew toys and spare himself unnecessary corrections for normal puppy mishaps.

Gated, however, does not mean unsupervised. Dalmatian puppies are active and exuberant, and require attention and activity to keep them out of mischief. If he must be unattended, use his crate.

GROOMING TOOLS

Dalmatians are considered "easykeepers." You don't need a battery of combs and brushes to keep them tidy. A slicker brush and a grooming glove are the only implements needed to maintain a clean and shiny coat. Introduce your puppy to grooming with a soft bristle brush early on so he learns to like it. It also helps condition the pup to hands-on attention, which will be invaluable when you have to clean his teeth and ears and clip his nails.

HOUSEHOLD HAZARDS

After puppy shopping, you must puppy-proof your house. Dalmatian pups are naturally curious critters that will investigate every-thing new, then seek-and-destroy just because it's fun. The message here is: Never let your puppy roam your house unsupervised. Scout your house for the following hazards.

Trash cans and diaper pails are natural puppy magnets (they know where the good stuff is!).

Medication bottles, cleaning materials, roach and rodent poisons and all other household chemicals should be locked up. You'll be amazed at what a deter-mined puppy can find.

Electrical cords must be unplugged wherever and whenever possible, and made inaccessible to the pup at all times. Injuries from chewed electrical cords are extremely common in young dogs.

Stringy stuff like dental floss, yarn and needles and thread are invitations to intestinal nightmares! Puppies snuffling about at ground level will find and ingest the tiniest of objects and will end up in surgery. Most vets will gladly tell you stories about the stuff they've surgically removed from puppies' stomachs.

Toilet bowl cleaners, if you have them, should be discarded immediately. Throw them out now. All dogs are born with "toilet sonar" and quickly discover

Don't forget the toys! All dogs need to chew, and puppies especially appreciate something soft (and safe) to sink their aching teeth into during the teething period.

that the water there is always cold.

Antifreeze, fertilizers and other potentially deadly stuff in your garage must be placed out of the reach of your Dal's nose and mouth. Antifreeze, sweet-tasting and attractive to dogs, is extremely toxic and just a few tasty drops will kill an adult Dalmatian, even less

for a pup. Lock it up well out of reach.

The items on your bedroom floor that belong in the closet or the hamper should go there. This means socks, stockings, underwear, shoes and slippers. Get them off the floor, put them away and close your closet doors. Puppies love all of the above because they smell just like you—multiplied by 200! You know that the dog's nose is thousands of times better than your nose—so imagine the olfactory feast he's enjoying with one of your shirts or socks!

SOCIALIZATION

This actually puppy-proofs your puppy, not your house. Puppy socialization is your Dalmatian's insurance policy to happy, stable adulthood, and is, without question, the most important element in a Dalmatian puppy's intro-duction to the human world.

When Dalmatians enter adolescence, they can become overly rambunc-tious and challenge the most patient of owners. They must be socialized before they can interact calmly with children. Thus, it is most important to expose them to new people and new situations at an early age. Canine research has proven that unsocialized pups grow up to be spooky and insecure, and fearful of people, children and strange places. Many turn into fear biters or become aggressive with other dogs, strangers, even family members. Such dogs can seldom be rehabili-tated and often end up abandoned in animal shelters. Dalmatian rescue groups tell horror stories about Dals that enter the rescue program every year. Puppy socialization lays the foundation for a well-behaved adult canine, thus preventing those canine behaviors that lead to abandonment and, in worst cases, euthanasia.

The primary social-ization period occurs during puppy's first 20 weeks of life. Once he leaves the safety of his mom and litter-mates at eight to ten weeks of age, your job begins. Start with a quiet, uncomplicated household for the first day or two, and then gradually introduce him to the sights and sounds of his new where there are crowds of people. Set a goal of two new places a week for the next two months. Keep

A sturdy fence of sufficient height is mandatory for your yard. Don't underestimate the Dal's athleticism; construct a fence that really will make it impossible for him to escape.

human world. Frequent interaction with children, new people and other dogs are essential at this age. Visit new places (dog-friendly, of course) like parks or even the local grocery store parking lot these new situations pleasant and upbeat, which will create a positive attitude toward future encounters.

"Positive" is especially important when visiting your veterinarian. You don't want a pup that quakes with fear every time he sets a paw inside his doctor's office. Make sure your vet is a true dog lover as well as a good dog doctor.

Your puppy also will need supervised exposure to children. Dalmatians are by nature good with children, but both dog and child must learn how to behave properly with each other. Puppies of all breeds tend to view little people as littermates and will exert the upper paw (a dominance ploy) over the child. Dalmatians are happy bundles of energy that could unintentionally overwhelm a small child during play. Children must be taught how to properly play with the dog and to respect his privacy. Likewise, adult family members should supervise and teach the puppy not to nip or jump up on the kids.

Take your Dalmatian youngster to puppy school. Some classes accept pups from 10 to 12 weeks of age, with one series of puppy shots as a health requirement. The younger the pup, the easier it is to shape good behavior patterns. A good puppy class teaches proper canine social etiquette rather than rigid obedience skills. Your puppy will meet and play with young dogs of other breeds, and you will learn about the positive

The key to harmony in a multi-pet household is to keep the introductions low-key and let the animals get to know each other on their own terms. It helps if they are introduced when young.

teaching tools you'll need to train your pup. Puppy class is important for both novice and experienced puppy folks. If you're a smart Dalmatian owner, you won't stop there and will continue on with a basic obedience class. Of course, you want the best-behaved Dalmatian in the neighborhood.

Remember this: There is a direct correlation between the quality and amount of time you spend with your puppy during his first 20 weeks of life and the character of the adult dog

Every new owner's favorite image: a sleeping Dal puppy. It's just a matter of hours until this toddler is back to his never-ending exploration of the world.

that he will become. You cannot recapture this valuable learning period, so invest the effort now and make the most of it.

WELCOMING THE DALMATIAN

Overview

- Purchase the essentials before the pup comes home! You're going to need food, bowls, a collar and ID tags, toys, a leash and collar, a crate, a slicker brush and grooming glove and more.
- Make your home safe for your puppy by removing hazards from the dog's environment.
- Socialization is critical to your puppy's proper development. Be proactive by introducing him to children and other dogs. Keep new experiences positive and fun.
- Try a puppy class as a way to socialize and get to know your new pup.

Dalmatian Puppy Kindergarten

The Dalmatian puppy is love, all wrapped up in a spotted fur coat. He is also a bundle of energy that needs substantial physical exercise and mental stimulation. Highly intelligent and eager to please, he is also strong-willed. Puppy classes, basic obedience and daily training sessions are necessary to channel these qualities into proper canine behavior. Your Dal needs to learn that you are now the top dog, the alpha person in his life. The sooner he understands

The calm before the storm...Inside that adorable package is a whirlwind of puppy curiosity and energy that needs to be directed in acceptable ways.

that, the fewer behavior problems you will encounter with your puppy and adult Dalmatian.

All dogs are pack animals and, as such, they need a leader. Your Dalmatian's first boss was his mother, now it's you. How best to teach him you are now the big Kahuna in his life? Puppy kindergarten starts the day you bring your puppy home.

Love your Dalmatian and he will love you back! Develop a bond with your Dal when he first comes home, as this will make him easier to train and will foster a closer relationship for the dog's entire life.

Before your puppy left his breeder, all of his life lessons came from his mom and littermates. When he played too rough or nipped too hard, his siblings cried and stopped the game. When he got pushy or obnoxious, his mother cuffed him gently with a maternal paw. Now his human family has to communicate appropriate behavior in terms his little canine mind will understand.

When you start the teaching process, keep this thought uppermost: The first 20 weeks of any canine's life are his most valuable

While your puppy was at the breeder's home, his dam served as pack leader for the litter. Once he comes home, you assume that role.

Dalmatian

learning time, a period when his mind is best able to soak up every lesson, both positive and negative. Positive experiences and proper socialization during this period is critical to his future development and stability. We'll learn more

Enforce the rules with your pup early on. Will he be allowed on the furniture or not? Make up your mind and stick to it; consistency is the key.

about socialization later, but know this: The amount and quality of time you invest with your Dalmatian youngster now will

determine what kind of an adult he will become. A wild dog, or a gentleman or lady? A well-behaved or naughty fellow? It's up to you.

Canine behavioral science tells us that any behavior that is rewarded will be repeated (this is called positive reinforcement). If something good happens, like a tasty treat or hugs and kisses, puppy will naturally want to repeat the behavior. That same research also has proven that one of the best ways to a puppy's mind is through his stomach. Never underestimate the power of a treat!

This leads to another very important puppy rule: Keep your pockets full of treats at all times, so you are prepared to reinforce good behavior whenever it occurs. That same "catch him in the act" principle also applies to negative behavior, or what we humans (not the dog) might consider negative (like digging in the trash can, which the dog or puppy does not know is "wrong"). If the pup gets into the garbage, steals food or does anything else that makes him feel good, he will do it again. What better reason to keep a sharp eye on your puppy to prevent these normal canine behaviors?

You and your puppy are beginning Puppy Class 101. Rule number one: Puppy must learn that you are now the alpha dog and his new pack leader. Rule number two: You have to teach him in a manner he will under-stand (sorry, barking just won't do it). Remember always that he knows nothing about human standards of behavior.

WORD ASSOCIATION

Use the same word (command) for each behavior every time you teach it, adding food rewards and verbal praise to reinforce the positive. Your pup will make the connection and will be motivated to repeat the behavior when he hears those key words. For example, when teaching the pup to void outside, use the

Your Dal looks up to you and trusts that you will provide him with a safe home, good care and proper guidance. Be a worthy leader.

same potty term ("Go potty," "Get busy" or "Hurry up" are commonly used) each time he eliminates, adding a "Good boy!" while he's urinating or eliminating. The pup will soon learn what those trips outside are for.

TIMING

All dogs learn their lessons in the present tense. You have to catch him in the act (good or bad) in order to dispense rewards or discipline. You have three to five seconds to connect with him or he will not understand what he did wrong. Thus, timing and consistency are your keys to success in teaching any new behaviors or correcting bad behaviors.

Successful puppy training depends on several important principles:

1. Use simple one-word commands and say them only once. Otherwise, the puppy learns that "Come" (or "Sit" or "Down") is a three- or four-word command. Never tell your dog to "Come," then correct him for something he did wrong. He will think the correction is for coming to you. (Think like a dog, remember?) Always go to the dog to stop unwanted behavior, but be sure you catch him in the act or the correction will not be understood.

2. Never correct your dog for something he did minutes earlier. Three to five seconds, remember? Never hit or kick your dog or strike him with a newspaper or other object. Such abusive measures will only create fear and confusion in your dog and could provoke aggressive behavior down the road.

3. Always praise (and offer a treat) as soon as he does something good (or stops doing something naughty). How else will the puppy know that he's a good dog? When praising or correcting, use your best doggie voice. Use a light and happy voice for praise, and a firm, sharp voice for warnings or corrections. A pleading, whiny "No, No" or "Drop that" will not sound too

convincing, nor will a deep, gruff voice make your puppy feel like he's a good dog. Your dog also will respond accordingly to family arguments. If couch to watch TV today, then scold him for climbing on the couch tomorrow.

Given the Dalmatian's intelligence and strong desire

You're sure to experience some ups and downs in raising your Dal pup, but one thing is undeniable— he's a charmer!

there's a shouting match, he will think that he did something wrong and head for cover. So never argue in front of the kids...or the dog!

4. Be consistent. You can't snuggle together on the to please his owner, he is a good student who learns quickly. Thus, puppy kindergarten and ongoing lessons in obedience are the best course to keeping his stubborn streak under control.

PUPPY GAMES

Puppy games are a great way to entertain your puppy and yourself, while subliminally teaching lessons in the course of having fun. Start with a game plan and a pocketful of tasty dog treats. Keep your games short so you don't push his attention span beyond normal Dalmatian puppy limits.

"Puppy catch-me" helps teach the come command. With two people sitting on the floor about 10 or 15 feet apart, one person holds and pets the pup while the other calls him, "Puppy, puppy, come!" in a happy voice. When the pup comes

running, lavish him with big hugs and give a tasty treat. Repeat back and forth several times…don't overdo it.

You can add a ball or toy and toss it back and forth for the puppy to retrieve. When he picks it up, praise and hug some more, give him a goodie to release the toy, then toss it back to person number two. Repeat as before.

Hide-and-seek is another game that teaches "Come." Play this game outdoors in your yard or another confined safe area. When the pup is distracted, hide behind a tree. Peek out to see when he discovers you are gone and comes running back to find you (trust me, he will do that). As soon as he gets close, come out, squat down with arms outstretched and call him "Puppy, come!" This is also an excellent bonding aid and teaches your puppy to depend on you.

"Where's your toy?" is a

Visit your pet shop for fun, safe, interactive toys.

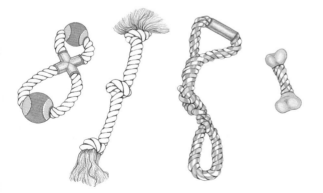

favorite of all sporting dogs, of which the Dal is definitely a relation. Start by placing one of his favorite toys in plain sight and ask your puppy "Where's your toy?" and let him take it. Then place your puppy safely outside the room and place the toy where only part of it shows. Bring him back and ask the same question. Praise highly when he finds it. Repeat several times. Finally, conceal the toy completely and let you puppy sniff it out. Trust his nose…he will find his toy.

Dalmatian puppies love to have fun with their people. Set aside an hour every day

Teaching your pup to bring you his toy is a precursor to playing retrieving games with your Dal as he gets older.

to interact with your Dal. Games are excellent teaching aids and one of the best ways to say "I love you" to your puppy.

DALMATIAN PUPPY KINDERGARTEN

Overview

- The Dalmatian is a pack animal, like all other dogs, and needs a leader to guide and instruct him.
- Positive reinforcement, punctuated with treats, is the best way to train any dog, especially one as intelligent and eager to please as the Dalmatian.
- Know the basic rules of puppy classes: You are alpha and your dog doesn't speak English.
- Word association, timing and consistency are three key lessons for Dal and owner.
- Learn the basic principles of successful puppy training.
- Play games with your puppy to help him learn to come when called.

House-training Your Dalmatian

Successful house-training should be your primary focus after you bring your Dalmatian puppy home. Use your puppy's crate and your common dog sense, and your pup will soon master the basics of Potty-training 101. Canines are natural den creatures, thanks to the thousands of years their ancestors spent living in caves and cavities in the ground, so puppies adapt quite naturally to crate confinement. Puppies are inherently clean little fellows and they prefer not to soil their "dens" or living spaces, which makes the crate a natural house-training aid.

Puppies want to stay clean; it's control they lack. Crate-training helps puppies establish a regular schedule and develop the muscle control they need to eliminate at the proper times and in the proper places.

Thus, your puppy's crate is actually a multi-purpose dog accessory: your Dalmatian's personal doghouse within your house, a humane house-training tool, a security measure that will protect your puppy as well as your household when you're not home, a travel aid to house and protect your dog when on the road (most motels will accept a crated dog) and, finally, a comfy dog space for your puppy when your anti-dog relatives come to visit.

For a housebroken Dal, the crate door can be left open when the owners are at home, allowing the dog to enter and exit as he pleases. Many dogs choose to spend time each day relaxing in their crates.

Some experienced breeders insist on crate use after their puppies leave, and a few even crate-train their pups before they send them home. But it's more likely that your Dalmatian has never seen a crate, so it's up to you to make sure his introduction is a pleasant one.

Introduce the crate as soon as your puppy comes home so he learns that this is his new "house." For the first

If you don't have a yard to accommodate your Dal's needs, you will have to take him out on his leash for regular exercise and relief trips.

day or two, toss a tiny treat into the crate to entice him to go in. Pick a crate command, such as "Kennel," "Inside" or "Crate," and use it every time he enters. You also can feed his first few meals inside the crate with the door still open, so his crate association will be a happy one.

Your puppy should sleep in his crate from his very first night. He may whine or object to the confinement. Be strong and stay the course. If you release him when he cries, you provide his first life lesson: "If I cry, I get out and maybe hugged." Not a good plan after all! A better idea is to place the crate next to your bed at night for the first few weeks. Your presence will comfort him, and you'll also know if he needs a middle-of-the-night potty trip. Whatever you do, do not lend comfort by taking the puppy into bed with you. To a dog, on the bed means he is your equal, which is not a good idea this early on.

Make a practice of placing your puppy in his crate for naps, at nighttime and whenever you are unable to watch him closely. Not to worry…he will let you know when he wakes up and needs a potty trip. If he falls asleep under the table and wakes up when you're not near him, guess what he'll do first? Make a puddle, then toddle over to say "Hi!"

Become a Dalmatian vigilante. Routines, consistency and an eagle eye are your keys to house-training success. Puppies always "go" when they wake up (quickly now!), after eating, after play periods, and after periods of confinement. Most pups under 12 weeks of age will need to eliminate at least every hour or so, or up to 10 times a day. (Set your kitchen timer to remind you.)

Always take your puppy outside to the same area, telling him "Outside" as you go out. Pick a potty phrase (such as "Hurry up," "Go potty" or "Get busy") and use it when he does his business, saying "Good puppy, hurry up!" Always use the same exit door for these potty trips, and confine the puppy to the room with the exit door area so he can find it when he needs it. Watch for sniffing and circling, sure signs he needs to relieve himself. Don't allow him to roam the house until he's fully house-trained…how will he find that outside door if he's three or four rooms away? He does not have a house map in his head.

Of course, he will have potty accidents. All puppies do. If you catch him in the act, clap your hands loudly, say "Aaah! Aaah!" and scoop him up to go outside. Your voice should startle him and make him stop. Be sure to praise when he finishes his duty outside.

If you discover the piddle spot after the fact…more than a few seconds later…you're too

Essential to a clean and happy life with your Dal is house-training him as a puppy. All dogs must be taught proper toileting habits.

late. Dogs only understand *in the moment* and will not understand a correction given more than five seconds (that's only *five*) after the deed. Correcting any later will only cause fear and confusion. Just forget it and vow to be more vigilant.

Never rub your puppy's nose in his mistake or strike your puppy or adult dog with your hand, a newspaper or other object to correct him. He will not understand and will only become fearful of the person who is hitting him.

House-training hint: before he is housebroken, remove puppy's water after 7 p.m. at night to aid in nighttime bladder control. If he gets thirsty, offer him an ice cube. Then just watch him race for the refrigerator when he hears the rattle of the ice cube tray!

Despite its many benefits, the crate can be abused. Puppies under 12 weeks of age should never be confined for more than two hours at a time, unless, of course, they are sleeping. A general rule of thumb is three hours maximum for a three-month-old pup, four or five hours for the four- to five-month-old, and no more than six hours for dogs over six months of age. If you're unable to be home to release the dog, arrange for a relative, neighbor or dog-sitter to let him out to exercise and potty.

One final, but most important, rule of crate use: never, *ever*, use the crate for punishment. Successful crate use depends on your puppy's positive association with his "house." If the crate represents punishment or "bad-dog stuff," he will resist using it as his safe place. Sure, you can crate your pup after he has sorted through the trash. Just don't do it in an angry fashion and never tell him "Bad dog! Crate!"

If you are unable to use a crate for house-training, or prefer to paper-train your Dalmatian pup, the routine is basically the same. Assign an out-of-the-way elimination place and cover it with newspaper. Take your puppy to the designated papered area on schedule. Use the specified potty word, and praise when he does his business. Do not use the area for any other purpose except potty breaks. Keep the area clean. You can place a small piece of soiled paper on the clean ones to remind the puppy why he's there. His nose will tell him what to do! You will have to consider, though, if this will be a viable method when your Dal is grown.

If you are still crate-shy,

what do you do with an uncrated puppy when you're not home? (Not a wise choice for a Dalmatian puppy.) Confine him to one area with a dog-proof barrier. Puppy-proofing alone may not be enough, even in a stripped environment. Some bored pups will chew through drywall. An exercise pen 4 feet by 4 feet square (available through pet suppliers), sturdy enough that pup can't knock it down, will provide safe containment for short periods. Paper one area for elimination, with perhaps a blanket in the opposite corner for napping.

Provide safe chew toys to keep him occupied, but even that is risky at best. If you don't or won't crate-train and cannot supervise your pup, be prepared to deal with the consequences.

Most importantly, remember that successful house-training revolves around consistency, repetition and word association. Maintain a strict schedule and use your key words consistently. It's no surprise that well-trained owners have well-trained Dalmatian pups.

HOUSE-TRAINING YOUR DALMATIAN

Overview

- The first challenge for all puppy owners is housebreaking, teaching the dog clean indoor behavior.
- The crate is the best answer to house-training your Dalmatian. Learn how to use a crate, not abuse it.
- Teach a relief command so that your puppy will always indicate when he needs to go out.
- Before housebreaking is complete, monitor your pup's water intake, especially at night.
- Never use the crate for punishment; the crate is pup's "house."
- Consistency is the key to establishing your Dal's daily toileting routine.

Teaching Basic Commands

Despite the Dalmatian's stubborn streak, he is a people-pleaser who is smart and eager to learn. Use positive teaching methods and set consistent limits to teach your Dal appropriate behavior. Start his puppy lessons as soon as he comes home. Research has proven that the earlier you begin, the easier the process and the more successful you both will be. Always work with your puppy in a quiet, distraction-free environment. Once your Dalmatian pup has mastered any task, change

The Dal's intelligence shines through in his expression. He makes a bright student who wants to please the owner he loves.

the setting and practice in a different location...another room or the yard. Then practice with another person or a dog nearby. If the pup reacts to the new distraction and does not perform the exercise, back up and continue with the exercise by removing the distractions for a while.

Take time out for fun! Keep your Dal attentive and interested in your training sessions by giving short positive lessons with playtime in between.

Appoint one person to instruct your puppy in the early stages so as not to confuse the pup. It's the too-many-cooks rule of dog training. Once your puppy has learned a command reliably, other family members can join in.

Ignore your Dalmatian for a few minutes before each training session. The lack of stimulation will make him more eager for your company and attention. Keep lessons short so your puppy won't get bored or lose his enthusiasm. This is especially important with a puppy that shows signs of boredom and lack of attention.

All dogs need an education in the basic commands to become polite canine citizens at home and in public.

Always keep your training sessions positive and upbeat. Use lots of praise, praise and more praise. Never train your puppy or adult dog if you are in a grumpy mood. You will lose patience, and he will think it is his fault. That will reverse any progress the two of you have made. Finish every training session on a positive note. If you have been struggling or unsuc-cessful, switch gears and do something he knows well (like "sit") and end the session.

Before you can teach your puppy any command, two things must happen. The puppy must learn to respond to his name (name recognition) and you must be able to gain and hold his attention. How to accomplish that? Why, with treats, of course! Treats are defined as tiny non-beef tidbits, preferably soft easy-to-chew treats. We don't want to over-feed this pup. Healthy dog treats broken into small pieces work well, and so do pieces of peanut butter breakfast cereal.

MAKE TRAINING A "CLICK"

Clicker training is a recent dog-training method. This can begin as early as eight weeks old and involves clicking a clicker, which is faster than verbal praise, when the dog does something that you want him to do. After the click, the dog is reinforced with a food treat. In the beginning, you wait for the pup to do what you want, such as sitting, then immediately click and feed a treat. No words are said; just the sound of the click signals to the dog that he has done something that deserves a treat. Eventually, when the pup catches on that sitting is good, you add the word "sit" after you click and give the treat.

ATTENTION AND NAME RECOGNITION

Start by calling your Dalmatian puppy's name. Once. Not two or three times, but once. Otherwise, he will think he has a three-part name and will ignore you when you say it once. Begin by using his name when he is not distracted and you know that he will look at you, and pop him a treat as soon as he looks at you. Repeat at least a dozen times, several times a day. It won't take more than a

done," "Free" and "Relax" are the ones most commonly recommended, although many people use "Okay" without a problem. You'll need this release word to tell your Dalmatian that an exercise is over and it's okay for him to relax or move from a stationary position.

Your Dal must be reliable with the come command. For his safety, you always want him to come to you when you call.

day or so before he understands that his name means something good to eat.

ESTABLISH A RELEASE COMMAND

That's the word you'll use to tell him the exercise is over, similar to "At ease" in the military. "All

COME COMMAND

This command has life-saving potential…preventing your Dalmatian from running into the street or after a squirrel, chasing behind a child on a bike, the list goes on and on. Always practice this command on leash. You can't afford to risk failure, or your pup will learn he does not have to come when called. You want your pup to respond reliably *every* time. Once you have your pup's attention, call him from a short distance, "Puppy, come!" (use your happy voice!) and give a treat when he comes to you. If he hesitates, tug him to you gently with his leash. Grasp

To teach the sit exercise, you may have to guide your dog into the proper position a few times until he gets the idea.

and hold his collar with one hand as you dispense the treat. This is important. You will eventually phase out the

treat and switch to hands-on praise only. This maneuver also connects holding his collar with coming and getting a treat, which will assist you in countless future behaviors.

Do 10 or 12 repetitions, 2 or 3 times a day. Once your pup has mastered the come exercise, continue to practice daily to burn this most important behavior into his tiny brain. Experienced Dalmatian owners know, however, that one can never completely trust a dog to come when called if the dog is bent on some self-appointed mission. Off-leash is often synonymous with out of control and, sadly, out of sight.

Ongoing practice in obedience is actually a lifetime dog rule, especially for a strong-willed Dalmatian. Dogs will be dogs, and if we don't maintain their skills, they will sink back into sloppy, inattentive behaviors that will be harder to correct. Incorporate all of these commands into your daily routine, and your dog will remain a gentleman of whom you can be proud.

SIT COMMAND

This one's a snap, since your Dalmatian already understands the treat process. Stand in front of your pup, move the treat directly over his nose and slowly move it backwards. As he folds backwards to reach the goodie, his rear will move downward to the floor. If the puppy raises up to reach the treat, just lower it a bit. The moment his behind touches the floor, tell him "Sit." (that's one word: "Sit.") Release the treat and gently grasp that collar as you did with "Come." He will again make that positive connection between the treat, the sit position and the collar hold.

As he becomes more proficient, make him hold the sit position longer before you give the treat (the beginning of the stay command). Start using your release word to release him from the sit position. Practice using the sit command for everyday activities such as sitting for his food bowl or a toy. Do random sits throughout the day, always for a food or praise reward.

STAY COMMAND

"Stay" is really just an extension of "Sit," which your Dalmatian already knows.

The sit/stay, like any command, is first taught on lead. The command is issued with the word "stay," accompanied by your outstretched hand as a "stop sign."

With your puppy sitting when commanded, place the palm of your hand in front of his nose and tell him "Stay." Count to five. Give him his release word and lots of praise. Stretch out the stays in tiny increments of time, making allowances for puppy energy. Once he stays reliably, move your body one step backward, then forward again. Gradually extend the time and distance that you move away. If the puppy moves from his stay position, say "No" and move up to stand in front of him. Use sensible timelines, depending on your puppy's attention span.

DOWN COMMAND

Down can be a tough command to master. Because the down is a submissive posture, take-charge breeds like the Dalmatian may find it especially difficult. That's why it's most important to teach it to your pup when he's very young.

From the sit position, move the food lure from his nose to the ground and slightly away from him between his front paws. Wiggle it as necessary. As soon as his front legs and rear end hit the floor, give the treat and tell him "Down, good boy, down," thus connecting the word to the behavior. Be patient, and be generous with the praise when he cooperates. Once he goes into the down position with ease, incorporate "Stay" as you did with "Sit." By six months of age, your puppy should be able to do a solid "Sit/Stay" for ten minutes, ditto for a "Down/Stay."

WAIT COMMAND

You'll love this one, especially when your Dalmatian comes into the house with wet or muddy paws. Work on the wait command with a closed door. Start to open the door as if to go through or out. When your dog tries to follow, step in front and body-block him to prevent his passage. Don't use the wait command just yet, just keep blocking until he gives up and you can open the door a little to pass through. Then say "Exit" and let him go through the door. Repeat by body-blocking until he understands and waits for you, then start applying the command "Wait" to the behavior. Practice in different doorways, using outside entrances (to safe or enclosed areas) only after he will wait reliably.

HEEL COMMAND

The actual heel command comes a bit later in the learning curve. A young Dalmatian should be taught simply to walk politely on a leash, at or near your side. This is best accomplished when your pup is very young and small, instead of 30 or 40 pounds (or more!) pulling you down the street.

Start leash training as soon as your pup comes home. Simply attach the leash to his buckle collar and let him drag it around for a little while every day. If he chews

You can teach your dog to stay in the down position in the same manner as you taught the sit/stay.

Dalmatian

All dogs, pet and show alike, must learn the heel command. Here, a show dog behaves well on lead while demonstrating his gait in the ring.

his leash, distract him with play activities or spray the leash with a product designed to make it taste unpleasant. Pet shops sell doggie deterrents for this purpose. Play a puppy game with the leash on. Make wearing his leash a happy moment in his day.

After a few days, gather up the leash in a distraction-free zone in the house or yard and take just a few steps together.

Hold a treat lure at your side to encourage puppy to walk next to you. Pat your knee and use a happy voice. Move forward just a few steps each time. Use the phrase "Let's go!" when you move forward, hold the treat at his nose level to keep him near, take a few steps and give the treat and praise!

Keep these sessions short and happy, a mere 30 seconds

at a time. Never scold or nag him into walking faster or slower, just encourage him with happy talk. Walk straight ahead at first, adding wide turns once he gets the hang of it. Progress to 90-degree turns, using a gentle leash tug, a happy verbal "Let's go!" and, of course, a treat. Walk in short 30- to 40-second bursts with happy breaks (use your release word) and brief play (hugs will do nicely) in between. Keep total training time short and always quit with success, even if just a few short steps. Formal heeling will come much later with advanced instruction in a basic obedience class.

All of the behaviors we've discussed are taught in some phase of a young-dog training class. Check with your vet or a local kennel club to find one in your area. There also are dozens of books that go into great detail about positive methods of obedience training for puppies and adults. You and your Dalmatian will both be smarter for your efforts.

TEACHING BASIC COMMANDS

Overview

- Begin basic obedience training on the right paw: select a quiet (distraction-free) environment, decide who will be the one person who trains the dog and keep lessons short and positive.
- Get your puppy's attention and maintain it.
- Teach name recognition and establish a release command.
- Use positive reinforcement, rewarding him with treats, praise and petting.
- The basic commands include come, sit, stay, down, heel and wait.
- Practice with your Dalmatian daily so that he becomes consistent 100% of the time.

DALMATIAN

Home Care for Your Dalmatian

Your dog will depend on you in sickness and in health. The more you know about canine health, the better prepared you'll be to handle everyday health issues and emergencies. Two issues are, without question, most important… weight control and dental hygiene.

WEIGHT CONTROL

To determine if your Dalmatian is overweight, you should be able to feel your dog's ribs beneath a thin layer of muscle with very gentle pressure on his rib cage. When viewing your dog from above,

Most dogs like to play in the grass, though grass allergies are fairly common in many dogs. Always keep an eye on your Dals' skin and coat.

you should be able to see a definite waistline and, from the side, he should have an obvious tuck-up in his abdomen.

Keep a record of his weight from each annual veterinary visit and watch for any changes in between check-ups. A few extra pounds? Adjust his food portions, perhaps switch to a "light," "senior" or lower calorie dog-food formula and increase his exercise. You should never feed your Dalmatian table scraps to avoid the risk of giving him purines that could harm his health.

Excessive weight is especially hard on older dogs with creaky joints. Walking and running (slower for old guys) are still the best workouts for health maintenance. Tailor your Dalmatian's exercise to fit his age and physical condition.

In between veterinary visits, you must keep your dog's teeth clean. Use a toothbrush and toothpaste made for dogs; feeding dry food and providing dental dog toys, designed to scrape away plaque as the dog chews, are other good measures.

The Dalmatian's body should be kept lean and muscular. Consider yourself as your Dal's personal trainer and dietitian.

DENTAL CARE

The American Veterinary Dental Society states that, by age three, 80 percent of dogs exhibit signs of gum disease. If neglected, these conditions will allow bacteria to accumulate in your dog's mouth and enter your dog's bloodstream through those damaged gums, increasing the risk for disease in vital organs such as the heart, liver and kidneys.

Your vet should examine your Dal's teeth and gums during his annual check-ups to make sure they are clean and healthy. During the other 364 days a year, you are your dog's dentist. Brush his teeth at least twice a week. Use a doggie toothbrush and use dog toothpaste flavored with chicken, beef or liver. (Minty people paste is harmful to dogs.) If your dog resists a toothbrush, try a nappy washcloth or gauze pad wrapped around your finger. Start the brushing process with gentle gum massages when your pup is young so he will learn to tolerate and even enjoy the process.

Feeding dry dog food is an excellent way to help minimize plaque accumulation. You can also treat your dog to a raw carrot every day. Carrots help scrub away plaque while providing extra vitamins A and C. Invest in healthy and safe chew objects, such as nylon or rubber bones and toys with ridges that act as tartar scrapers.

ROUTINE CHECKS

Your weekly grooming sessions should include body checks for lumps (cysts, warts and fatty tumors), hot spots and other skin or coat problems. Rub him down with your hands; don't rely on the brush to find abnormalities. Although harmless lumps under the skin are common in older dogs, many can be malignant, and your vet should examine any abnormality. Black, mole-like patches or growths on any body part, especially between the toes, require immediate veterinary inspection. Be extra-conscious of dry skin, a flaky coat and thinning hair, all signs of thyroid disease. Check for fleas and have annual stool cultures done to check for intestinal parasites, which can cause poor coat quality and intestinal problems, as well as weaken your dog's resistance.

Your Dalmatian's vision may deteriorate with age. A bluish haze is common in geriatric dogs and does not impair vision. However, always check with your vet about any changes in the eyes to determine if they are harmless or indicative of a problem.

How about his other end? Does he chew at his rear or scoot and rub it on the carpet? That's a sign of impacted anal glands. Have your vet express those glands (it's not a job for amateurs).

Kidney disease is a problem that can be treated

successfully with early diagnosis. Dogs seven years old and older should be tested annually for healthy kidney and liver function. If your dog

The Dal's eyes should be bright and clear, to match his sparkling personality!

drinks excessive amounts of water, urinates more frequently or has accidents in the house, run, don't walk, to your vet. Kidney failure can be managed with special diets to reduce the workload on the kidneys.

Heart disease is common in all canines. Symptoms include panting and shortness of breath, chronic coughing, especially at night or upon first waking in the morning, and changes in sleeping habits. Many forms of heart disease can be treated if you catch it early.

The moral here is...know your Dalmatian. Early detection of any problem is the key to your dog's longevity and quality of life.

In hot weather, be sure that your Dal has access to plenty of water and shade.

EMERGENCY CARE

Every dog owner should know the signs of an emergency. Many organizations sponsor canine first-aid seminars. Obvious emergencies include vomiting for more than 24 hours, bloody or prolonged (over 24 hours) diarrhea, fever (normal canine temperature is 101.5 degrees F), sudden swelling of the head or any body part (allergic reaction to an insect bite or other stimulus) or any symptoms of bloat, which require *immediate* veterinary attention. For Dalmatians, straining to urinate with very little elimination requires immediate veterinary attention.

Symptoms of other common emergency situations include:

Heatstroke—Excessive panting, drooling, rapid pulse, dark reddened gums and a frantic, glazed expression (you'll know it when you see it).

Hypothermia (wet dogs +

cold weather)—Shivering, very pale gums, and body temperature under 100 degrees F.

Shock—Severe blood loss from an injury can send a dog into shock. Symptoms include white gums, shivering, weak pulse, weakness and listlessness, depression and lowered body temperature.

Other symptoms that can be red flags for cancer or other serious health problems include: lumps or abnormal swelling; sores that do not heal; sudden or unexplainable weight loss; loss of appetite; unexplained bleeding or discharge; an offensive body odor; difficulty swallowing or eating; loss of stamina or reluctance to exercise; difficulty breathing, urinating or defecating; a bloated appearance and persistent stiffness or lameness.

Again, know your Dalmatian! Read about canine health care and be aware of even subtle changes in your Dalmatian. Keep a list of symptoms and remedies in a handy place to reference when necessary. Your Dalmatian's life could depend on it.

HOME CARE FOR YOUR DALMATIAN

Overview

- Weight control and dental care should be foremost on every Dalmatian owner's home-care routine. Obesity can shorten the life of your Dal, as can plaque accumulation and the diseases associated with it.
- During weekly grooming sessions, keep an eye on the condition of your Dalmatian's coat. Always watch for moles, bumps, lumps and parasites, all of which can lead to serious problems.
- Know the signs of wellness so that you can recognize when your Dalmatian's health may be compromised by disease.

Feeding Your Dalmatian

"Y ou are what you eat" is as true of dogs as it is of humans. To keep your Dalmatian in prime condition, feed a quality dog food that is appropriate for his breed, age and lifestyle.

Premium dog-food manufacturers have developed their formulas through strict quality controls, using only quality ingredients obtained from reliable sources. The labels on the food bags tell you what products are in the food (beef, chicken, corn, etc), with ingredients listed in descending order

The litter should nurse readily; their mother's milk provides the pups with the best nutrition for the first weeks of life.

of weight or amount in the food. Do not add your own supplements, "people food" or extra vitamins to the food. You will only upset the nutritional balance of the dog food, which could affect the growth pattern of your Dalmatian pup.

A hungry litter at dinnertime. The breeder starts the pup off on solid foods as a part of the weaning process.

The major dog-food brands now offer foods for every breed size, age and activity level. As with human infants, puppies require a diet different than that of an adult. The new growth formulas contain protein and fat levels that are appropriate for different-sized breeds. Large-breed, fast-growing dogs require less protein and fat during their early months of rapid growth, which is better for healthy joint development. Medium (your Dalmatian) and small breeds also have different nutritional requirements during their first year of growth.

No Dal turns down a treat! Don't overdo it, and make sure the treats you offer are Dalmatian-friendly (meaning low-purine).

Because Dalmatians have high uric acid secretion, they should not have excessive protein that is high in purines in their diets, nor should they have red meat. Most low-protein non-red-meat commercial diets are well tolerated, and extra proteins (as in high-protein "performance" diets, meat and table scraps) should be avoided. Too much protein and certain purines can lead to bladder and kidney stones. Urinary stones cause problems for many Dalmatians, and breeders warn owners to be aware of the connection of stone-forming and the dog's diet. Dalmatians *must* be fed a

Don't forget the water! Water is an essential component of the Dal's diet for good urinary-tract health. Many Dal owners supply only distilled water for their dogs to drink.

low-purine diet. Be aware of the following foods that yield high amounts of purine: organ meat (kidney, liver and brain), seafood (like anchovies, scallops, sardines, mackerel and herring), game meats (like venison and pheasant), sweetbreads and gravies. Consult your breeder and your veterinarian for healthy food choices for your Dal.

When and how much to feed? An eight-week-old puppy does best eating three times a day. (Tiny tummies, tiny meals.) At about 12 weeks of age, you can switch to twice-daily feeding. Most breeders suggest two meals a day for the life of the dog, regardless of breed.

Free-feeding, that is, leaving a bowl of food available all day, is not recommended. Free-feeding fosters picky eating habits…a bite here, a nibble there. Free-feeders also are more likely to become possessive of their food bowls. With scheduled meals, it's easier to predict elimination, which is the better road to house-training. Regular meals also help you know just how much puppy eats and when, valuable information if your pup gets sick.

Dry food is recommended by most vets, since the dry particles help remove plaque and tartar from the dog's teeth. The "food hog" who almost inhales his food will do better with a splash of water in his food pan. A bit of water added immediately before eating also is thought to enhance the flavor while preserving the dental benefits. Whether feeding wet or dry food, always have water available at all times, although gulping water at mealtimes can lead to bloat.

On that note, *do* get information about gastric torsion (bloat), its symptoms and preventatives. Deep-chested breeds are prone to this often-fatal condition, which can be avoided with daily precautions regarding feeding and exercise. The bottom line is this: What and how much you feed your dog is a major factor in his overall health and longevity. It's worth your investment in extra time and dollars to determine the best diet for your Dalmatian.

FEEDING YOUR DALMATIAN

Overview

- Quality counts when feeding the Dalmatian. Offering a top-quality dog food is the most reliable and convenient way to provide complete nutrition for your dog.
- Discuss with your vet and/or breeder low-purine foods for your Dal.
- Avoid free feeding, which can lead to picky eating, obesity or possessive behavior.
- Bloat is a life-threatening condition that affects deep-chested dogs. It is related to eating and feeding habits and is preventable.
- Your Dalmatian's health relies upon a proper diet.

Grooming Your Dalmatian

The Dalmatian's short, close-fitting coat is sleek and requires minimal upkeep to keep it glossy and healthy in appearance. However, "grooming" involves more than just brushing your dog's coat. Good grooming habits are an essential part of your Dal's total health-care program and should include his ears, teeth and nails, as well as thorough body checks for external parasites, lumps and bumps.

Hold your first grooming session as soon as your puppy has adjusted

Nail clipping is best begun as a puppy. You won't want to struggle with a grown Dalmatian who resists his pedicures.

to his new home base. Start with tiny increments of time, stroking him gently with a soft brush, briefly handling his paws, looking inside his ears, gently touching his gums. Use lots of sweet talk and offer little bits of dog treats during each session, so he'll think such personal contact is a prelude to a feast.

Dalmatians are prone to certain skin problems and can encounter irritants outdoors. Use grooming times to check your Dal's skin and coat thoroughly for any signs of a problem.

The Dalmatian coat is virtually groom-free. He has no thick undercoat, so shedding is not seasonal; rather, it occurs all year long. His short coat requires little more than a weekly brushing with a soft bristle brush or curry to remove dust, stimulate circulation and distribute oils in the skin. A rub-down with a chamois leather or a hound mitt (a rubber grooming glove) also works very well.

Use a cotton ball or soft wipe to clean your dog's ears. Only clean that which you can see; never enter the ear canal, as this can cause injury.

Although the coat requires little upkeep, the same is not true of the Dalmatian's living space, where his short hair affixes itself magnetically to every surface. House-proud owners will be challenged. Frequent bathing is seldom necessary, and, in fact, will remove the essential oils that keep your dog's skin supple and his coat soft and gleaming.

In between baths, a hose-down on a hot day will clean the coat and cool off the dog.

Of course, there are those times when a bath is necessary. To minimize the stress of bath time, start when your pup is small. Lure your puppy into the tub with the usual food rewards. Line the tub or stall with a towel for safe footing. Gradually add shallow water, and the bathing process begins. He may never learn to love it, but all you need is his cooperation.

When bathing, be sure to rinse the coat completely to prevent itching from residual shampoo. A good chamois is ideal for drying as it absorbs water like a sponge.

Because of their short coats, Dalmatians are easily chilled. They should be thoroughly dried and kept away from drafts for a good while after bathing and drying to prevent chilling.

Dental hygiene is as important for canines as it is for humans. Plaque and tartar build-up will lead to gum disease, which is a harbinger of more serious diseases. A daily tooth-brushing with products made for dogs is the ideal, but twice weekly may be more realistic.

Nails should be trimmed once a week. This is always the least favorite grooming chore. Early introduction will help make the clipping process easier. Offer those puppy treats with each clipping session. Nip off the nail tip or clip at the curved part of the nail. Be careful not to cut the quick (the pink vein in the nail), as that is quite painful, and the nail may bleed profusely. You can staunch the bleeding with a few drops of a clotting solution. Keep it on hand...accidents

happen.

Weekly ear checks are worth the proverbial pound of cure. Ear infections are common to all breeds of dog, with some Dals more prone to chronic ear infection than others. Regular cleansing will keep your dog's ears clean and odor-free.

Symptoms of ear infection include redness and/or swelling of the outer or inner ear, a nasty odor or a dark, waxy discharge. If your dog digs at his ear(s) with his paw, shakes his head a lot or appears to lose his balance, see your vet at once.

GROOMING YOUR DALMATIAN

Overview

- While the Dalmatian does not require much grooming, proper coat maintenance is a vital part of his overall health-care program.
- Be prepared to find Dalmatian hairs everywhere!
- The Dalmatian owner must tend to his dog's coat, teeth, nails and ears.
- You will only have to bathe your Dalmatian occasionally, probably two or three times per year.

CHAPTER 13

DALMATIAN

Keeping the Dalmatian Active

Dals are products of their working heritage and thus are blessed with high energy levels and incredible endurance. They require robust physical exercise every day to help maintain their physical and emotional health and happiness (yours, too!). Lively backyard play activities and lengthy, fast-paced, on-leash walks will keep the adult Dal mentally and physically fit. As with all breeds of dog, your Dal should never be allowed to run loose beyond a fenced-in area. Running at large presents a danger to the dog and to the neighborhood.

Once your Dal has reached 12 months of age, agility training can start. This is a fun and very active dog sport that the high-flying Dal is sure to enjoy.

How far and how long can you jog? Your adult Dal will handle as much running as you are able to provide. Most Dalmatians have almost limitless endurance and can easily outjog most owners. Limit the jogging of a young Dal and don't jog until he is about 9–10 months old so as not to break down the pasterns from the pounding of the jogging. A half-mile is recommended to start. A young Dalmatian's bones are relatively soft and his growth plates do not fully close until about 12 months of age. Thus, his musculoskeletal structure is more vulnerable to injury during that period and should not be subjected to heavy stress. That means no games that encourage twisting, high jumping or heavy impact on his front or rear quarters. Playtime with other puppies and older dogs should be supervised to avoid wrestling and twisting until your pup is past the danger age. Swimming, whenever possible, is excellent exercise.

Regular exercise keeps your Dal in fit, athletic condition. He will gladly accept as much exercise as you can give him.

Avoid strenuous exercise with your "Firehouse Pup." For the first year, he will get a lot of exercise just being a puppy!

When and where to walk is as important as how long. On warm days, avoid walking during midday heat and go out during the cooler morning or evening hours.

Those daily walks and exercise periods are also excellent bonding sessions. Your Dalmatian will look forward eagerly to his special time with you. As a creature of habit, your dog will bounce with joy when he sees you don your cap, pick up his leash or rattle your keys.

You can take your exercise program to another level. Plan a weekly night out with your Dalmatian and enroll in a class. Your Dal is a natural athlete and would enjoy, indeed thrive, on classes in obedience, maybe agility…or both! The benefits of obedience class are endless. You will be motivated to work with your dog daily so that the two of you don't look unprepared at each week's class. Your dog will have a grand old time, and so will you. You'll both be more active, and thus healthier. Your dog will learn the basics of obedience, will be better behaved and will become a model citizen.

Agility class offers even more healthy outlets for an active Dalmatian. Training for agility is not recommended until at least one year of age. He will learn to scale an A-frame ramp, race headlong through a tunnel, balance himself on a teeter-totter, jump up and off a platform, jump through a hoop and zig-zag between a line of posts. The challenge of learning to navigate these agility obstacles, and his success in mastering each one, will make you proud of both of you!

You can take both of these activities one step further and compete with your dog in obedience and agility competition. Trials are held year-round and are designed for all levels of experience. Find a club or join a training group. Check the DCA and AKC websites for details and contact people.

Dalmatians have yet another avenue in which to demonstrate their great endurance skills. They can earn the title of Road Dog (RD) by accompanying a human on horseback over a 12.5-mile course, performing commands along the way. The Road Dog Excellent (RDX) title requires a similar 25-mile run.

If you plan to show your Dalmatian in conformation, make sure you look for a show-quality puppy and discuss your goals with the breeder. Most local breed clubs host conformation training classes and can help a novice handler get started with his pup. As with other competitions, it's best to start when your Dalmatian is young so he develops a good "ring" attitude. Competition aside, your Dalmatian needs to be part of family activities and will be happiest when he is with people.

KEEPING THE DALMATIAN ACTIVE

Overview

- Structure an exercise regimen for your Dalmatian, allowing him daily walks and free running time in a safely enclosed area.
- Do not let young puppies exert themselves, as they are more prone to injury at a young age.
- Do not overdo exercise on warm days.
- Explore the different types of training, sports, competitions and shows with your Dal.

DALMATIAN

Your Dalmatian and His Vet

One of the first things you and your new puppy will do together is visit the veterinarian.

A good veterinarian is worth his weight in dog treats! The good vet dispenses more than shots and pills. He is also a wellness provider who will fashion a total health-care plan for your Dal and help you become a better canine health-care provider as well. Take your puppy to your veterinarian of choice within the first few days of bringing the puppy home. Show the vet any health records of shots and wormings from your breeder. The vet will conduct a thorough physical exam to make sure your Dalmatian is in good health and will work out a schedule for vaccinations, microchipping, routine medications and regular well-puppy visits. A good vet will be gentle and affectionate with a new pup and do everything possible to make sure the puppy is not frightened or intimidated. Your selection of a vet should be guided by whether or not the vet likes Dalmatians and knows Dalmatians. Since Dals have some unique health concerns, it pays to have a Dal-smart vet!

Your vet will keep a record of your dog's vital signs, including his temperature.

Vaccine protocol for puppies varies with many veterinarians, but the most common is a series of three "combination" shots given at three- to four-week intervals. Your puppy should have had his first shot before he left his breeder. "Combination" shots vary, and a single injection may contain five, six, seven, or even eight vaccines together. Many breeders and veterinarians feel the potency in high-combination vaccines can compromise a puppy's immature

The key to a happy and healthy dog is having a good relationship with your vet and keeping up with regular visits.

immune system, so they recommend fewer vaccines in one shot or even separating some of the vaccines into individual injections.

The wisest and most conservative course is to

You want your Dal always to be the active athlete he's meant to be, which means paying attention to the health of his bones and joints. Here the vet checks the hip joint for any looseness, which can signal dysplasia.

administer only one shot in a single visit, rather than two or three shots at the same time. That means extra trips to

your veterinarian with your puppy and adult dog, but your Dalmatian's healthy immune system is worth your time.

VACCINES

The vaccines recommended by the American Veterinary Medical Association (AVMA) are those that protect against the diseases most dangerous to your puppy and adult dog. Those include distemper (canine distemper virus— CDV), fatal in puppies; canine parvovirus (CPV or parvo) highly contagious and also fatal in puppies and at-risk dogs; canine adenovirus (CAV2), highly contagious and high risk for pups under 16 weeks of age; and canine hepatitis (CA1), highly conta- gious, with pups at high risk. These are generally combined into what is often called a five-way shot. Rabies immunization is required in all 50 states, with that vaccine given three weeks after completing the series of the puppy shots.

Vaccines no longer routinely recommended by the AVMA, except when the risk is present, are canine parainfluenza, leptospirosis, canine coronavirus, bordetella (canine cough) and Lyme disease (canine borreliosis). Your veterinarian will alert you if there is an incidence of these diseases in your town or neighborhood so you can vaccinate accordingly.

The AVMA guidelines issued in 2003 recommend vaccinating every three years instead of annually. Research suggests that annual vaccinations may actually be excessive and are linked to many of today's canine health problems. Mindful of that, the current AVMA guide on vaccinations also suggests that veterinarians and owners consider a dog's individual needs before they vaccinate. Many dog owners now do titer tests to check their dogs'

antibodies rather than automatically vaccinate for parvo or distemper.

Rabies vaccination is required of all dogs. However,

Dogs can suffer from pollen allergies just like humans. Flowers, weeds, grasses and the like can be itchy irritants to your Dal.

for many years the rabies vaccine has been available in a one-year and a three-year shot. Both offer the same protection, so why vaccinate every year?

Regardless of vaccine frequency, every Dalmatian

should visit his veterinarian once a year, more frequently as a pup and as a senior citizen. At the very least, he needs an annual heartworm test before he can receive another year of preventative medication. Most importantly, an annual visit keeps your vet apprised of your pet's health progress, and the hands-on exam often turns up small abnormalities that the average dog owner can't see or feel.

HEARTWORM

This is a parasite, a worm that propagates inside your dog's heart and will ultimately kill him. Now found in all 50 states, heartworm is delivered through a mosquito bite. All dogs living in rural areas should take heartworm preventative, which can be given daily or monthly in pill form, or in a shot given every six months. Heartworm preventative is a prescription medication available only

through your veterinarian. Ask your vet which heartworm medication he recommends.

FLEAS AND TICKS

Fleas have been around for centuries, and it's likely that you will wage flea battle sometime during your Dalmatian's lifetime. Fortunately today there are several low-toxic, effective weapons to aid you in your war against fleas. Find out about the most recent spot-on treatments, monthly pills and insect-growth regulators from your vet. Over-the-counter flea and tick collars offer minimal to limited protection. Homespun remedies include brewer's yeast, garlic, citronella and other herbal products, but none has been scientifically proven to be effective.

Lyme disease (canine borreliosis), ehrlichiosis and Rocky Mountain spotted fever are tick-borne diseases now found in almost every state and can affect humans as well as dogs. Dogs that live in or visit areas where ticks are present, whether seasonally or year-round, must be protected.

A well-informed dog owner is better prepared to raise a healthy dog. Always ask your vet what shots or medications your dog is getting and what they are for. Keep a notebook or dog diary, and record all health information so you won't forget it. Believe me, you will forget.

Fortunately, today's veterinary community is focused on preventative care and canine wellness as well as treating animals after they are sick. The American Holistic Veterinary Medical Association and other specialty groups now offer acupuncture, herbal remedies, homeopathy and other alternative therapies in addition to traditional disease treatment and prevention. Many pet owners today incorporate

both philosophies in their dogs' health-care programs.

SPAY/NEUTER

Let's address the spay/neuter question: Should you or shouldn't you? This is almost

Every dog needs to rest, but if your ever-active Dal seems to be less than his normal exuberant self, it may signal that he's not feeling well.

a non-question, since spay/neuter is the best health insurance policy you can give your Dalmatian. Statistics prove that females spayed before their first heat cycle (estrus) have a 90% less risk of several common female cancers and other serious female health problems. Males neutered before their male hormones kick in, usually before six months of age, enjoy zero to greatly reduced risk of testicular and prostate cancer and other related tumors and infections. Additionally, males will be less apt to roam, become aggressive or display those overt male behaviors that most people find annoying.

Altering your dog will not necessarily make him fat and lazy, and you need only to adjust his diet and increase exercise if weight gain does occur. Statistically, spay/neuter makes a positive contribution to pet overpopulation and, most importantly, to your dog's long-term health. The bottom line is: If you are keeping your Dal as a pet and not a show dog, it's the thing to do!

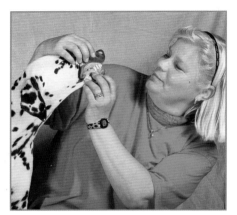

Dental care is extremely important and must not be overlooked as a part of a dog's routine care.

YOUR DALMATIAN AND HIS VET

Overview

- Upon bringing your Dal home, take him to the vet for an exam.
- Discuss a vaccination schedule with your vet.
- Heartworm threatens the lives of dogs, though it can be prevented through a prescription drug.
- Parasites like ticks and fleas can lead to various diseases that must be guarded against.
- Focus on preventative care for your Dal, not just treating illness.
- Spaying/neutering eliminates some undesirable sexually related behaviors while, most importantly, protecting your pet from various cancers and other conditions.